forget

Mind Games

MEMORY FUN

Facts, Trivia, and Quizzes

remember

Elsie Olson

Lerner Publications ◆ Minneapolis

Lerner Publications Company
A division of Lerner Publishing Group, Inc.
241 First Avenue North
Minneapolis, MN 55401 USA

For reading levels and more information, look up this title at www.lernerbooks.com.

Main body text set in Avenir LT Pro
Typeface provided by Linotype

Library of Congress Cataloging-in-Publication Data

The Cataloging-in-Publication Data for *Memory Fun: Facts, Trivia, and Quizzes* is on file at the Library of Congress.
ISBN 978-1-5124-3418-7 (lib. bdg.)
ISBN 978-1-5124-4941-9 (EB pdf)

Manufactured in the United States of America
1-42054-23924-3/8/2017

CONTENTS

Introduction
DO YOU REMEMBER...?

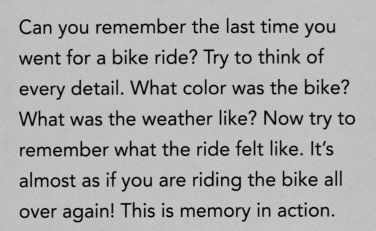

Can you remember the last time you went for a bike ride? Try to think of every detail. What color was the bike? What was the weather like? Now try to remember what the ride felt like. It's almost as if you are riding the bike all over again! This is memory in action.

memory

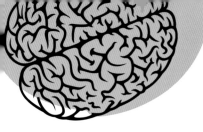

BRAIN FILES

Memory is the process of storing and **retrieving** information in your brain. Your memory tells the story of your life. And without memory, you would not be able to learn new information.

Everyone has a memory. But no one can remember everything. Why do you forget some things and not others? What can your memories tell you about yourself? Read on and find out!

Word Challenge: Part 1

Spend twenty seconds looking at the words below. Then, turn the page and keep reading. Your memory of these words will be tested at the end of this book!

anteater	dog
egg	peacock
pencil	school
notebook	airplane
tomato	computer
house	tulip

Chapter 1
ANCIENT MEMORIES

Memory played a very important role in ancient times. Before writing was invented, people shared information using stories. These stories were passed down for hundreds of years.

MEMORY PALACE

Roman philosopher Cicero studied memory in the 100s CE. He used a trick known as a memory palace. Cicero would think of a place he knew well, like the route home.

Cicero would picture the route. Then he would think of something he wanted to remember, like a list of people's names. He assigned each person's name to a location on the route. By retracing the route in his mind, Cicero could remember each name.

Build a Memory Palace! (Part 1)

Build a memory palace using your bedroom. On a separate sheet of paper, list five different spots in your room. Picture each spot you wrote down. Then look at the words below:

library book

teddy bear

astronaut

calculator

backpack

Assign each word to a different location in your room. Think of an image in your mind to relate the two. This could be the library book laying on your bed. Or an astronaut turning on your lamp. Got it? Turn the page and look for the Memory Palace Test!

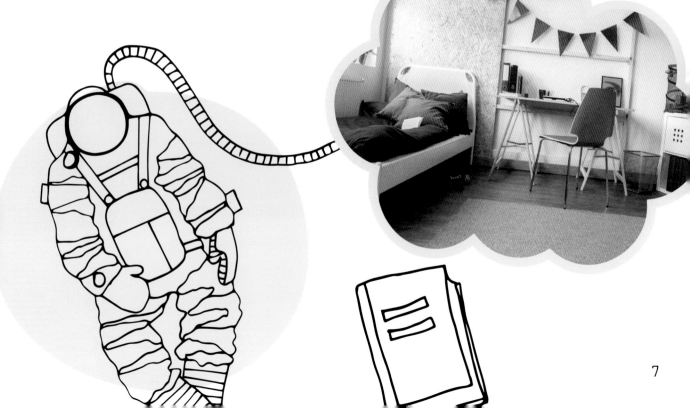

HOW MEMORY WORKS

A memory is a pattern of stored connections in your brain. These connections begin forming when your senses pick up on something.

Try to remember a time you ate pizza. Can you smell the cheese? Can you feel the pizza's warmth? These sensations traveled to a part of your brain called the **hippocampus**. The hippocampus decides whether a memory is worth storing.

Memory Palace Test!

Can you remember the words from page 7? Go through your memory palace. Picture each spot and the word assigned to it. Write down what you remember. Go back to page 7 to check your answers. How did you do?

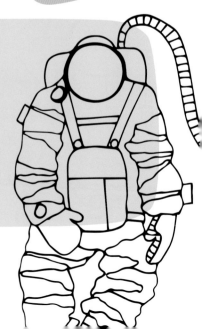

Mnemonic Device

Mnemonic devices are tools that help people remember things. One is creating a phrase based on what you are trying to remember. For example, *my very excellent mother just served us noodles* can help you remember the order of the eight planets. It is Mercury, Venus, Earth, Mars, Jupiter, Saturn, Uranus, Neptune. Look at the words below:

sedimentary

igneous

metamorphic

These are the three main types of rocks. Come up with a mnemonic device to remember them. Repeat it out loud five times. Now turn the page!

Mnemonic Device: Results!

Can you remember the three types of rocks without looking? Think of the mnemonic device you created on page 9!

MAKING A MEMORY

Before a memory is stored, it must be **encoded**. Your brain does this using chemical and electrical signals that travel between **neurons**. As these signals travel, they form paths called synapses. Each synapse contains a different detail of a memory. When they combine, you have a complete memory!

STRONG SYNAPSES

When you remember eating pizza, your brain **accesses** the synapses holding those details. It retrieves the memory. The more information that travels back and forth along a synapse, the stronger it becomes. So the more you think about your pizza, the stronger that memory is. Hungry yet?

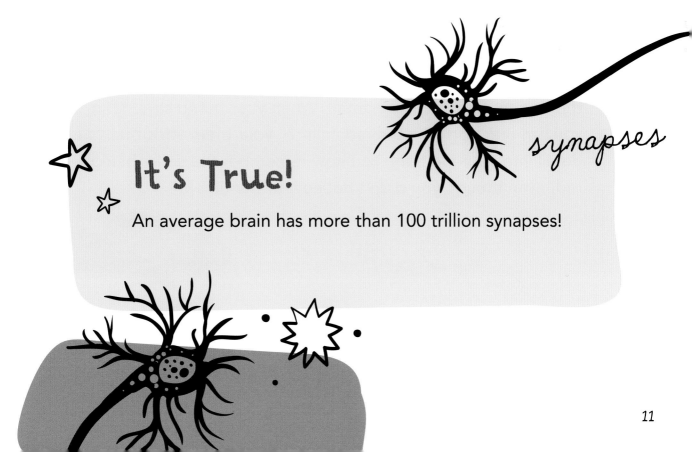

synapses

It's True!

An average brain has more than 100 trillion synapses!

MIXED MEMORIES

Have you ever seen the same movie as a friend, but you both remember it differently? Even if your brain stores a memory, it may not match what actually happened. Emotions surrounding an event can alter your memory of it. And new experiences can cause your brain to rewrite a past event.

MEMORY FILLERS

Your brain may also fill gaps in your memory with details. Imagine you and a friend see a dog run past. You remember the dog, but not its every detail. When your friend says, "Did you see that dog with the red collar?" your brain adds that detail into your memory. You now remember the collar being red, even though you didn't notice it at the time!

How Forgetful Are You?

Answer the questions below on a separate sheet of paper.
See how strong your memory is!

TRUE OR FALSE:

1. You have forgotten a close friend's birthday.

2. You can remember fewer than four lunches you ate last week.

3. You don't have any phone numbers memorized. (911 doesn't count!)

4. You have lost something in the last two weeks.

5. You have forgotten your homework at home in the last month.

Did you answer "true" to three or more questions? You may be forgetful.
Not to worry! Try using some of the memory tricks in this book, and you'll
be a memory marvel in no time.

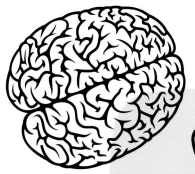

Chapter 3

SHORT-TERM MEMORY

When your brain encodes a memory, it must decide how long to store it. Most scientists believe that all memories begin as short-term memories. Your brain can store short-term memories for no more than thirty seconds. After thirty seconds, the memory is either lost or moved to long-term storage.

FILTER FUNCTION

Your brain filters information it decides isn't useful. For example, you might not remember the name of every kid in school. But you remembered the name of your teacher after the first day.

It's True!

sleep

Getting enough sleep and eating healthy food can help improve your memory.

Short-Term Memory Test

Stare at the images below for thirty seconds. Then turn the page to test your short-term memory!

Short-Term Memory Test: Results!

Gather a sheet of paper and a timer. Set the timer for one minute. Write down every object you can remember from page 15.

Check your answers against page 15. Give yourself a point for every correct object. Now, tally up your points!

9–12 points: Your short-term memory is sharp!

5–8 points: You have pretty average short-term memory.

Less than 5 points: Your short-term memory is not very strong. Try this activity again to strengthen it!

short-term
memory

SAVE THAT MEMORY!

Remember, only some short-term memories move to long-term storage. There are tricks you can try if you have a short-term memory you want to save. Reread written words, say something out loud many times, or look at an image again and again. These tricks can strengthen a memory and help you remember it.

Find the Face!

Which of these faces did you see on page 15?

Chapter 4
LONG-TERM MEMORY

Scientists believe the brain can store almost an unlimited number of long-term memories. However, if your brain stores too much information, it can become difficult for it to find memories. So it removes older or less useful memories. Because of this, memories usually get worse over time.

AUTOMATIC MEMORIES

Long-term memories can be divided into two different categories. **Automatic** memories are those you can remember without really thinking about them. These are often skills. For example, you know how to brush your teeth without thinking about the action each time.

SPECIFIC MEMORIES

Some memories are tied to specific experiences. You need to think about these memories to recall them. They could be events or facts. For example, if you think about it, you might remember your fifth birthday party or that the capital of Texas is Austin.

$$x + y =$$

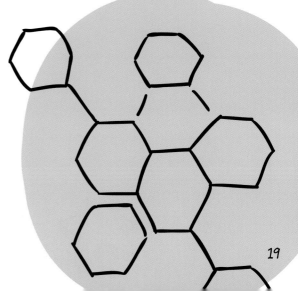

How Good Is Your Long-Term Memory?

Answer the questions below. Use your finger to follow the path. Learn about your long-term memory skills!

Can you remember a gift you got for your seventh birthday?

no

yes

Can you remember the name of the first movie you saw in the theater?

yes

no

Can you remember the last movie you saw in the theater?

Can you remember five or more classmates from your kindergarten class?

yes

no

yes

no

You might consider a career as a spy. Your memory is top-notch!

You have a decent memory!

You may not be a memory all-star, but your memory isn't too shabby!

It might not be a bad idea to keep a diary.

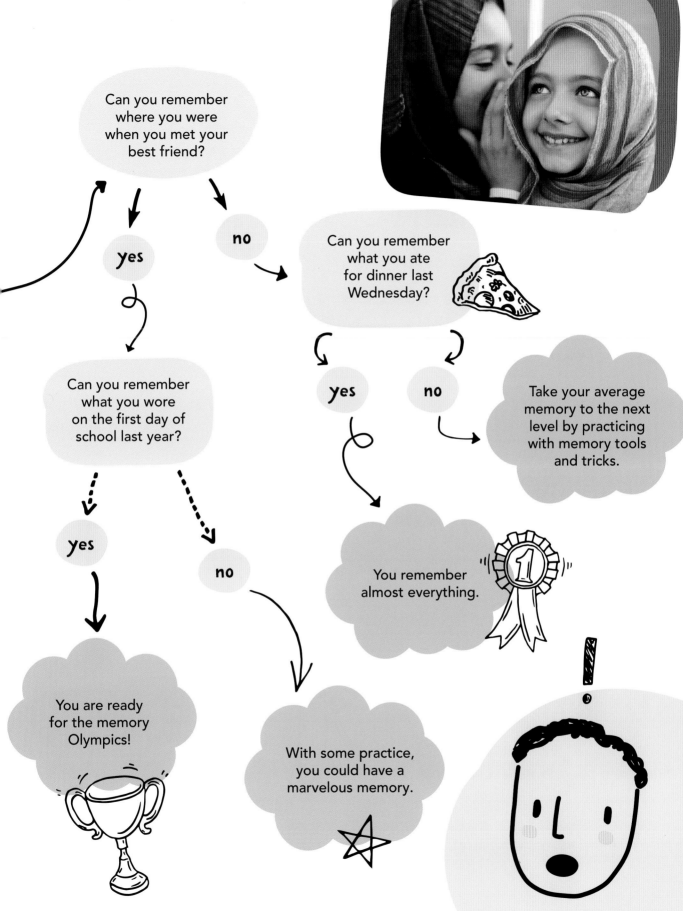

Can you remember where you were when you met your best friend?

yes

no

Can you remember what you ate for dinner last Wednesday?

Can you remember what you wore on the first day of school last year?

yes

no

Take your average memory to the next level by practicing with memory tools and tricks.

yes

no

You remember almost everything.

You are ready for the memory Olympics!

With some practice, you could have a marvelous memory.

Chapter 5

AMAZING MEMORY!

Some people have **remarkable** memories. They can remember long strings of numbers or even memorize entire books! Others can remember detailed images.

PHOTOGRAPHIC MEMORY

People with a photographic memory claim to be able to take a mental snapshot of a scene and remember its details perfectly. Scientists have not proven that this skill exists. But that doesn't mean some people don't remember images **incredibly** well!

photographic memory

EIDETIC MEMORY

Eidetic memory is similar to photographic memory, but it is more short term. People with this skill can remember an image in detail after looking at it for only seconds. However, the memory lasts only a few minutes. Scientists have proven that eidetic memories exist. Up to 15 percent of kids have this skill.

Do You Have an Eidetic Memory?

Stare at the photo below for ten seconds. Then turn the page to test your eidetic memory!

Do You Have an Eidetic Memory? Results!

On a separate sheet of paper, write down all the details you can remember about the photo on the previous page. When you are done, flip back to page 23. Compare your notes to the image. How did you do?

EXTREME MEMORIES

Some people with **amazing** memories can remember their own past. There is a woman known as AJ who has this skill. AJ can remember nearly every detail of her life from the time she was eleven years old! When asked about a specific date, she can remember what she ate for dinner that day or what happened on a TV show she watched.

amnesia

It's True!

Some people's memories are amazing because of what they can't remember. Total or partial memory loss is known as amnesia. Most amnesia is caused by some type of brain injury.

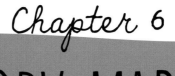

Chapter 6

MEMORY MARVELS

Are you a memory whiz? Or do you have trouble remembering what you ate for lunch today? Either way, your memories can tell you a lot about yourself.

Word Challenge: Part 2

Think back to the list of words you studied in the Introduction. On a separate sheet of paper, write down all the words you can remember. Check your list against page 5. Give yourself one point for each word you got right. Tally your score. How strong was your memory?

9-12 correct: Your memory is super strong!

5-8 correct: Remembering this many words after reading so much text is no small feat.

0-4 correct: Your memory could be stronger. Keep playing memory games to improve your skills.

EXPLORE MORE!

Memories are just one method of self-understanding. There are many fun ways you can learn more about your personality and preferences. Explore personality tests, dream interpretation, and more. Find out what makes you *you*!

Memory Magic!

Test your friends' memories with these fun games!

What's Missing?

Materials:

- clean table
- 20 objects of various sizes such as dice, game pieces, or school supplies
- stopwatch or timer

Step 1: With your friends in another room, arrange the objects on the table.

Step 2: Bring your friends back into the room. Allow them to look at the objects for one minute. Then ask them to leave the room again.

Step 3: Remove two objects, and invite your friends back in. Can they identify which objects are now missing?

Step 4: Do the activity again, this time taking away two different objects. Then try a third time. Do your friends get better or worse each round? What does this tell you about memory?

Memory Card Pickup

Materials:

- one complete deck of playing cards
- table

Step 1: Choose twelve pairs out of the deck of cards. These could be pairs of twos, eights, jacks, etc. Set the rest of the cards aside.

Step 2: Shuffle the twelve pairs. Then lay them face-down on the table.

Step 3: Take turns turning two cards over at a time. If you get a pair, pick up those cards. If you don't, turn the cards back over. Play until all the cards are picked up.

Step 4: The player with the most cards wins.

GLOSSARY

accesses: enters, approaches, or gets information from

amazing: very impressive and perhaps hard to believe

automatic: done without your thinking about it

encoded: converted from one system of communication into another

hippocampus: a curved, elongated ridge in the brain that consists of gray matter and is involved in forming, storing, and processing memory

incredibly: in an unbelievable or amazing manner

neurons: nerve cells that carry information between the brain and other parts of the body

remarkable: extraordinary or worth noticing

retrieving: locating something, such as information, and bringing it back to mind

FURTHER INFORMATION

Memory Boosters

http://www.scholastic.com/teachers/article/memory-boosters

Try some of these tips and tricks to help improve your memory!

Memory Experiments

https://faculty.washington.edu/chudler/chmemory.html

Test your memory with these experiments designed especially for kids!

Memory Matters

http://kidshealth.org/en/kids/memory.html

Learn all about memory and how it works on this cool website.

Moore, Gareth. *Think Outside the Box*. Minneapolis, MN: Hungry Tomato, 2016.

A super-sharp memory will help you complete the fun puzzles and activities in this book.

Swanson, Jennifer. *Brain Games: The Mind-Blowing Science of Your Amazing Brain*. Washington, DC: National Geographic Kids, 2015.

Test the power of your mind with memory games and other brain busters.

INDEX

Photo Acknowledgments

The images in this book are used with the permission of: Design elements and doodles © advent/Shutterstock.com, anyaivanova/Shutterstock.com, Fears/Shutterstock.com, IgorKrapar/Shutterstock.com, kostolom3000/Shutterstock.com, mhatzapa/Shutterstock.com, Mighty Media, Inc., Mjosedesign/Shutterstock.com, Natasha Pankina/Shutterstock.com, Nikolaeva/Shutterstock.com, Photoraidz/Shutterstock.com, primiaou/Shutterstock.com, Sashatigar/Shutterstock.com, Vector Tradition/Shutterstock.com, whitemomo/Shutterstock.com, and YegoeVdo22/Shutterstock.com; © FGorgun/iStockphoto.com, p. 1 (top); © TBD/iStockphoto.com, p. 1 (bottom); © gbh007/iStockphoto.com, p. 4 (top); © monkeybusinessimages/iStockphoto.com, pp. 4 (bottom), 14, 19 (bottom); © kcslagle/iStockphoto.com, p. 5; © Cris Foto/Shutterstock.com, p. 6; © KatarzynaBialasiewicz/iStockphoto.com, p. 7; © MarianVejcik/iStockphoto.com, p. 8; © Mari/iStockphoto.com, p. 9 (top); © LindaYolanda/iStockphoto.com, p. 9 (bottom); © PeopleImages/iStockphoto.com, p. 10; © shironosov/iStockphoto.com, p. 11; © andresr/iStockphoto.com, p. 12 (top); © Geiger/Shutterstock.com, p. 12 (bottom); © Pavel L Photo and Video/Shutterstock.com, p. 13; © Ruslan Guzov/Shutterstock.com, pp. 15 (top), 17 (top, middle); © Djomas/Shutterstock.com, p. 15 (cat); © Brian A Jackson/Shutterstock.com, p. 15 (pumpkin); © vitaliy_73/Shutterstock.com, p. 15 (mittens); © Irina Fischer/Shutterstock.com, p. 15 (ice cream cone); © docent/Shutterstock.com, p. 15 (clock); © Pruser/Shutterstock.com, p. 15 (apple); © DenisMArt/Shutterstock.com, p. 15 (notebook); © Everything/Shutterstock.com, p. 15 (shoes); © korkai HD/Shutterstock.com, p. 15 (teddy bear); © Tanor/Shutterstock.com, p. 15 (hamburger); © Floortje/iStockphoto.com, p. 15 (flowerpot); © urfin/Shutterstock.com, p. 15 (pencil); © RichLegg/iStockphoto.com, p. 16; © Rawpixel.com/Shutterstock.com, p. 17 (top, left); © champja/iStockphoto.com, p. 17 (top, right); © Fertnig/iStockphoto.com, p. 17 (bottom, left); © Lapina/Shutterstock.com, p. 17 (bottom, right); © VaLiza/Shutterstock.com, p. 18 (left); © perkmeup/iStockphoto.com, p. 18 (right); © iofoto/iStockphoto.com, p. 19 (top); © Heijo/iStockphoto.com, p. 20; © Zurijeta/iStockphoto.com, p. 21; © risteski goce/Shutterstock.com, p. 22; © bowdenimages/iStockphoto.com, p. 23 (top); © gorillaimages/Shutterstock.com, p. 23 (bottom); © kali9/iStockphoto.com, p. 24; © drbimages/iStockphoto.com, pp. 25, 27 (top); © gilaxia/iStockphoto.com, p. 26; © malerapaso/iStockphoto.com, p. 27 (bottom); © shironosov/iStockphoto.com, p. 29; © Monkey Business Images/Shutterstock.com, p. 31.

Front cover: © PeopleImages/iStockphoto.com (top, left); © TBD/iStockphoto.com (top, middle); © FGorgun/iStockphoto.com (top, right); © fatihhoca/iStockphoto.com (bottom, right).

Back cover: © monkeybusinessimages/iStockphoto.com (top); © drbimages/iStockphoto.com (middle); © FGorgun/iStockphoto.com (bottom).